FOR MY LITTLE FOODIES...
GRACE AND MILES

D1716043

 HI!

It's me,
Little Belly Monster!

Do you know what a belly monster's favorite thing is in the whole world?

FOOD!

Delicious, good-for-my-belly food.

Even talking about
food is making
me hungry.
That's where I
need your help.
What can I eat that's
yummy for my tummy?

GRUMBLE 〉〉

〉〉 RUMBLE

That's a great idea!
I can help make it, too.

And with a little help
from a grown up,
so can you. Come on,
I'll show you!

First,
we ALWAYS
start by washing
our hands.

Then,
we get all the
ingredients
together.

For the pizza, we'll need...

WHOLE WHEAT PITA BREAD

PIZZA SAUCE

& LIGHT MOZZARELLA CHEESE

Next, we get our favorite toppings. I like...

HAM

RED PEPPER

& PINEAPPLE

Mmm... so good together.

WHOLE WHEAT PITA BREAD

Now we can start.
Put a piece of
whole wheat pita
bread on the table.

PIZZA SAUCE

Use a spoon to put some pizza sauce on the pita and spread it all around. Don't forget to leave room for the crust!

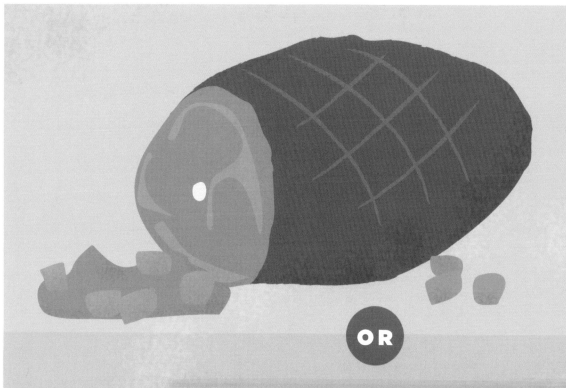

OR

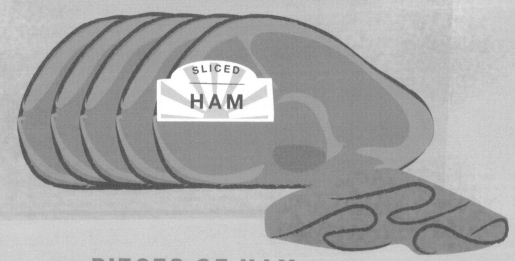

SLICED
HAM

PIECES OF HAM

Add a few
pieces of ham.
We'll need space
for other tasty
toppings, too.

PINEAPPLE

OR

TIDBITS

PINEAPPLE CHUNKS

Put chunks of pineapple on...

My favorite!

One for you...

one for me...

*DICED **RED PEPPER**

Drop on bits of
diced* red pepper.
Mumo Belly helps
me cut them.

*DICED means cut into small chunks.

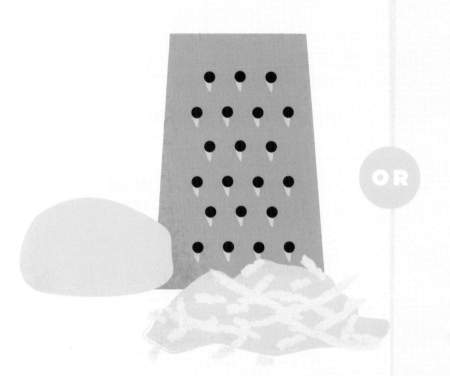

SHREDDED
CHEESE!

SHREDDED LIGHT MOZZARELLA CHEESE

Sprinkle* shredded
light mozzarella cheese
over everything but
the crust.

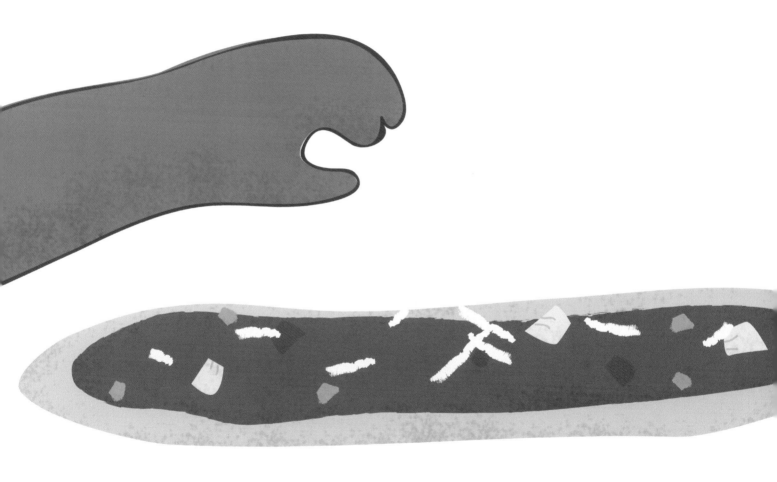

 *SPRINKLE means drop a little bit at a time, all around.

HOT OVEN AT 375°F/190°C

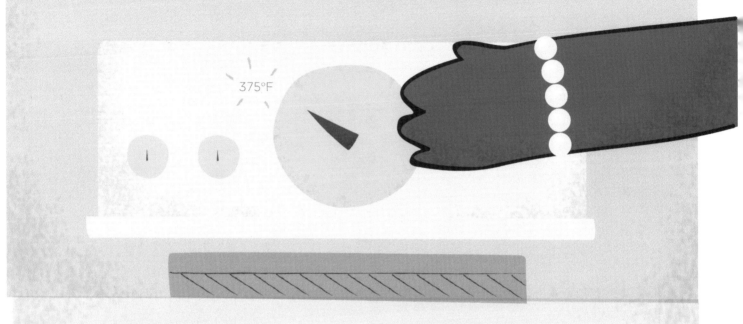

375°F

11

FOR 11 MINUTES

We're getting close... now we just have to bake it! Mumo Belly puts it in the hot oven✚ for me. We wait for 11 minutes. Or until the cheese is ooey gooey.

Is it ready yet?

...Now?

... What about now?

✚SAFETY: I never touch the oven by myself!

PIZZA!

And then...

WE EAT!

Mmm…

LITTLE BELLY MONSTER PIZZA!

CHOMP

CHOMP

CHOMP

That was fun.
Thanks for helping
me fill my belly
with yummy food.
So... what are we
going to make next?

BURP

Excuse me.

OTHER TASTY TOPPINGS

If you want to try something different,
you can add or change the toppings.

MEAT

Try cooked chicken, cooked
turkey or even no meat!

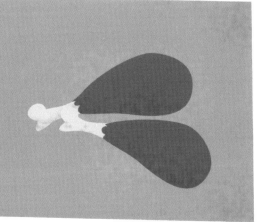

VEGETABLES

Try mushrooms,
yellow peppers or spinach.
Tasty.

ADD DIFFERENT CHEESES

Like feta or goat cheese. Mmm...

Or try anything else you think could taste good on a pizza.

DON'T FORGET
THE VEGGIES!

SHOPPING LIST

- ☐ WHOLE WHEAT PITA BREAD
- ☐ PIZZA SAUCE
- ☐ HAM

- [ ] **RED PEPPER**

- [ ] **PINEAPPLE**

- [ ] **LIGHT MOZZARELLA CHEESE**

Eat with you again soon!

COOKING NOTES

Dave, thank you for believing in me and for doing things that I didn't think
were possible. Love always.

With special thanks to Sarah, Judy, Steph, Lisa and all my amazing family
and friends who helped make this happen.

Text Designed by: Steph Mackie

Website: littlebellymonster.com   Email: books@littlebellymonster.com

Publisher's Notes:
This cookbook requires adult supervision and is not meant for children
to do on their own. The publisher cannot accept liability for any resulting
injury, damage or loss to persons or property, however they may arise.

RUMBLE
GRUMBLE

CPSIA information can be obtained
at www.ICGtesting.com
Printed in the USA
248580LV00008B

9 780986 942402